W9-CYF-038

# WYOMING

Sarah Tieck

## VISIT US AT
### www.abdopublishing.com

Published by ABDO Publishing Company, PO Box 398166, Minneapolis, MN 55439.

Printed in the United States of America, North Mankato, Minnesota.
062012
092012

 PRINTED ON RECYCLED PAPER

Coordinating Series Editor: Rochelle Baltzer
Contributing Editors: Megan M. Gunderson, Marcia Zappa
Graphic Design: Adam Craven
Cover Photograph: *iStockphoto*: ©iStockphoto.com/KenCanning.
Interior Photographs/Illustrations: *Alamy*: John Elk III (p. 11), Andre Jenny (pp. 11, 26, 27), Dennis McDonald (p. 25); *AP Photo*: White House Handout, David Bohrer (p. 23), Alex Brandon (p. 23), Casper Star-Tribune, Kerry Huller (p. 27); *Getty Images*: MPI (p. 13); *iStockphoto*: ©iStockphoto.com/PhilAugustavo (p. 19), ©iStockphoto. com/CrackerClips (p. 19), ©iStockphoto.com/Nnehring (p. 30), ©iStockphoto.com/outtakes (p. 30); *Shutterstock*: Steve Bower (p. 29), EastVillage Images (p. 21), Lane V. Erickson (p. 26), kavram (p. 17), Catherine Lall (p. 21), Mary Lane (pp. 5, 9), Philip Lange (p. 30), Steve Shoup (p. 30), Videowokart (p. 27).

All population figures taken from the 2010 US census.

### Library of Congress Cataloging-in-Publication Data

Tieck, Sarah, 1976-
 Wyoming / Sarah Tieck.
   p. cm. -- (Explore the United States)
 ISBN 978-1-61783-390-8
 1. Wyoming--Juvenile literature. I. Title.
 F761.3.T49 2013
 978.7--dc23
                          2012018272

# WYOMING

# Contents

# ONE NATION

The United States is a **diverse** country. It has farmland, cities, coasts, and mountains. Its people come from many different backgrounds. And, its history covers more than 200 years.

Today the country includes 50 states. Wyoming is one of these states. Let's learn more about this state and its story!

**Did You Know?**

Wyoming became a state on July 10, 1890. It was the forty-fourth state to join the nation.

4

Wyoming's name refers to its wide-open land. It comes from a Native American word that means "upon the great plain."

5

# Wyoming Up Close

The United States has four main **regions**. Wyoming is in the West.

Wyoming has six states on its borders. Montana is north. South Dakota and Nebraska are east. Colorado is south. Utah is southwest and Idaho is west.

Wyoming has a total area of 97,812 square miles (253,332 sq km). It is the least populated state. About 564,000 people live there.

# REGIONS OF THE UNITED STATES

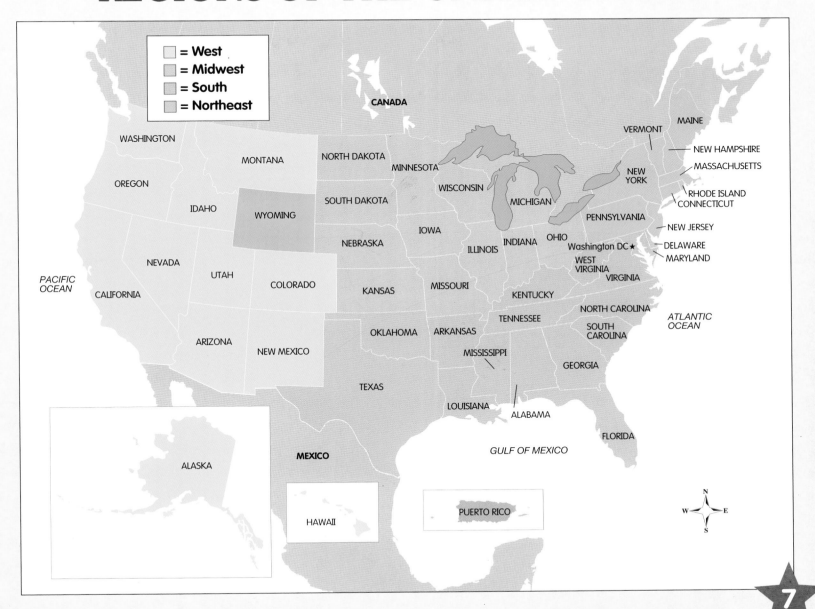

= West
= Midwest
= South
= Northeast

CANADA

WASHINGTON
MONTANA
NORTH DAKOTA
MINNESOTA
VERMONT
MAINE
NEW HAMPSHIRE
MASSACHUSETTS
OREGON
IDAHO
WYOMING
SOUTH DAKOTA
WISCONSIN
NEW YORK
MICHIGAN
RHODE ISLAND
CONNECTICUT
PENNSYLVANIA
NEVADA
UTAH
COLORADO
IOWA
NEBRASKA
ILLINOIS
INDIANA
OHIO
Washington DC ★
NEW JERSEY
DELAWARE
MARYLAND
WEST VIRGINIA
VIRGINIA
PACIFIC OCEAN
CALIFORNIA
KANSAS
MISSOURI
KENTUCKY
NORTH CAROLINA
ATLANTIC OCEAN
TENNESSEE
ARIZONA
NEW MEXICO
OKLAHOMA
ARKANSAS
SOUTH CAROLINA
MISSISSIPPI
GEORGIA
TEXAS
LOUISIANA
ALABAMA
FLORIDA
GULF OF MEXICO
MEXICO
ALASKA
HAWAII
PUERTO RICO

N
W E
S

7

# IMPORTANT CITIES

Cheyenne (sheye-AN) is Wyoming's **capital**. It is also the state's largest city, with 59,466 people. It is on Crow Creek and Dry Creek.

Cheyenne is a center for business. Large companies such as Taco John's are based there. And, the city is close to an air force base.

## Wyoming

Casper●

Laramie●
Cheyenne★

The Wyoming State Capitol was completed in 1888.

Casper is Wyoming's second-largest city. It is home to 55,316 people. It is on the North Platte River, near the Laramie Mountains.

Laramie is the state's third-largest city, with 30,816 people. It is located on the Laramie River. Many people visit the city to hike, ski, and do other outdoor activities.

The city of Casper is at the foot of Casper Mountain.

Laramie has a historic downtown.

11

# Wyoming in History

Wyoming's history includes Native Americans and settlers. Native Americans have lived in present-day Wyoming for thousands of years.

In 1803, President Thomas Jefferson bought land in the **Louisiana Purchase**. This included most of Wyoming. In the 1860s and 1870s, miners and farmers moved to the area. Then in 1890, Wyoming became a state.

Fort Laramie provided supplies for settlers. Soldiers also used this important fort. And, Pony Express riders stopped there.

# Timeline

**1834**

Fort William was built. It later became Fort Laramie.

**1890**

Wyoming became the forty-fourth state on July 10.

1800s

Yellowstone National Park became the first national park in the United States.

Devils Tower National Monument became the country's first national monument.

**1872**

**1906**

14

**1924**

Nellie Tayloe Ross was elected governor of Wyoming. She was the first female governor in the United States.

**2012**

The Wyoming State Fair honored 100 years.

1900s

2000s

Fires swept through parts of Yellowstone National Park. This was the largest known fire in the park's history.

Wyoming state quarters started being made.

**2007**

**1988**

# Across the Land

Wyoming has mountains, hills, forests, valleys, **canyons**, and grassy, flat land. The Rocky Mountains cover much of the state. Parts of the Missouri, Colorado, and Columbia river systems start in the mountains. The state is home to several national parks and forests.

Many types of animals make their homes in Wyoming. These include bison, pronghorn, and bald eagles.

**Did You Know?**

In July, the average temperature in Wyoming is 67°F (19°C). In January, it is 19°F (-7°C).

The Lower Falls of the Yellowstone River is just one of Wyoming's many waterfalls.

# EARNING A LIVING

Wyoming has important businesses. Many people work in service jobs, such as helping visitors to the state. Some work for the government. Others work for factories that **process** the state's natural **resources**.

Wyoming has many natural resources. Oil, coal, and natural gas come from its land. Beef cattle and other livestock are raised in the state. Farmers produce hay and sugar beets.

Many people come to Wyoming to see its natural areas. Geysers are popular with visitors.

Farmers use special machines to collect sugar beets and other crops.

# Natural Wonder

Yellowstone National Park is in parts of Wyoming, Idaho, and Montana. It became the first US national park in 1872. It covers more than 2 million acres (800,000 ha) of land.

The park is known for its **geysers**. It is home to hundreds of them! Yellowstone also features mountains, forests, waterfalls, hot springs, and **canyons**. People visit the park to hike, camp, and fish.

Minerals in hot springs create interesting colors in the land.

Yellowstone National Park is home to pronghorn, moose, coyotes, bighorn sheep, and even bears!

21

# HOMETOWN HEROES

Many famous people have lived in Wyoming. Dick Cheney was born in Nebraska in 1941. He grew up in Casper. Later, he served in the US House of Representatives.

From 2001 to 2009, Cheney was vice president of the United States. He served with President George W. Bush. He was the first person from Wyoming to reach such a high national office.

★★★★★★★★★★★★★★★★★★★★

Cheney enjoys fly-fishing in Wyoming's rivers.

★★★★★★★★★★★★★★★★★★★★★★★

Cheney has many connections to Wyoming. He attended the University of Wyoming. And his wife, Lynne, is from this state.

23

Esther Hobart Morris was born in New York in 1814. In 1869, she moved to South Pass City. In 1870, she became the country's first female **justice of the peace**.

Morris was a leader in women's voting rights. In 1869, she helped get a law passed to allow women to vote in the Wyoming Territory. In 1890, because of that law, Wyoming became the first state to allow women to vote.

### Did You Know?

Wyoming is called "the Equality State." That's because women there were the first in the United States to get equal rights!

Statues at the Wyoming State Capitol (*right*) and the US Capitol honor Morris.

# Tour Book

Do you want to go to Wyoming? If you visit the state, here are some places to go and things to do!

## ⭐ Remember

Stop by Fort Laramie National Historic Site. Visitors can see some of the fort's original buildings. The fort started as a fur-trading center and became a military post in the late 1840s.

## ⭐ Explore

Go camping in Grand Teton National Park. The park features snow-capped mountains, forests, and the famous Jenny Lake.

## ⭐ Play

See a rodeo at Cheyenne Frontier Days. This event takes place every July.

## ⭐ See

Drive along Wind River Canyon near Thermopolis. Cliffs rise more than 2,000 feet (600 m) above the river!

## ⭐ Discover

Watch Old Faithful in Yellowstone National Park. This geyser has sprayed every 30 to 120 minutes for more than 80 years!

# A GREAT STATE

The story of Wyoming is important to the United States. The people and places that make up this state offer something special to the country. Together with all the states, Wyoming helps make the United States great.

Devils Tower National Monument is one of Wyoming's natural wonders. This special rock formation is 867 feet (264 m) tall.

# Fast Facts

**Date of Statehood:**
July 10, 1890

**Population (rank):**
563,626
(50th most-populated state)

**Total Area (rank):**
97,812 square miles
(9th largest state)

**Motto:**
"Equal Rights"

**Nickname:**
Equality State

**State Capital:**
Cheyenne

**Flag:**

**Flower:** Indian paintbrush

**Postal Abbreviation:**
WY

**Tree:** Eastern Cottonwood

**Bird:** Western Meadowlark

# Important Words

**canyon**  a long, narrow valley between two cliffs.
**capital**  a city where government leaders meet.
**diverse**  made up of things that are different from each other.
**fort**  a building with strong walls to guard against enemies.
**geyser**  (GEYE-zuhr)  a spring that shoots out hot water and steam.
**justice of the peace**  a local official who has the power to decide minor court cases, give oaths, and marry people.
**Louisiana Purchase**  land the United States purchased from France in 1803. It extended from the Mississippi River to the Rocky Mountains and from Canada through the Gulf of Mexico.
**process**  to change something by taking it through a set of actions.
**region**  a large part of a country that is different from other parts.
**resource**  a supply of something useful or valued.

# Web Sites

To learn more about Wyoming, visit ABDO Publishing Company online. Web sites about Wyoming are featured on our Book Links page. These links are routinely monitored and updated to provide the most current information available.

**www.abdopublishing.com**

# Index